YAZOO

LEVEL 3
Pupils' Book

T0385809

**Charlotte Covill Jeanne Perrett
with Tessa Lochowski**

PEARSON
Longman

Yazoo 3 — Contents

2

THE YAZOO BAND

3 _____

4 _____

1 _____

2 _____

1 Write the names.

2 Sing along with the band.

Hello, girls and boys,
Hello to you.
We are the animals in the zoo.
We're your friends and we are here.
We're learning English all the year.

Hello, girls and boys,
Hello to you.
We're your friends here in the zoo.
We like songs and books and fun.
Let's learn English, everyone!

Hello, girls and boys,
Hello to you.
Welcome to our zoo!

5 _____

6 _____

7 _____

8 _____

5

My classroom

1 **Look, count and write. Then ask and answer.**

__3__ bags
_____ pencils
_____ pens
_____ computers
_____ books
_____ rubbers
_____ desks
_____ chairs
_____ rulers
_____ pencil cases
_____ crayons

How many bags?

Three.

2 **Ask and spell.**

How do you spell 'book'?   B-O-O-K.

3 **Play the game.**

Simon says 'Sit down'.

open your book
sit down
listen   be quiet
stand up   close your
write book
read

Numbers 1–100

1 **Listen, point and say.** •))

10 ten   **20** twenty   **30** thirty   **40** forty   **50** fifty

60 sixty   **70** seventy   **80** eighty   **90** ninety   **100** one hundred

2 **Listen and match.** •))

21   33   44   52   65   76   87   99

thirty-three   fifty-two   sixty-five   eighty-seven   twenty-one
ninety-nine   seventy-six   forty-four

3 **Read and circle.**

1 forty-four   43   (44)   24

2 thirty-nine   69   29   39

3 twenty-one   21   31   41

4 eighty-six   84   85   86

5 sixty-seven   77   67   76

6 fifty-four   54   64   45

4 **Do the sums and write.**

1 20 + 6 = __26__   twenty-____six____
2 50 + 9 = _____   _____–nine
3 40 + 5 = _____   forty-_____
4 90 + 2 = _____   _____–two
5 30 + 4 = _____   _____–four

Days of the week and time

1 **Listen, point and say.** •))

Monday	Tuesday	Wednesday	Thursday	Friday	Saturday	Sunday

2 **Look at 1. Listen and point. Then answer.** •))   What's for lunch?

3 **Look at 1. Ask and answer.**

fish   burger   spaghetti   soup   potatoes   salad   bread   chips   pizza   eggs   cheese sandwiches   sausages   chicken   salad

It's Monday.
What's for lunch?

Chicken and
spaghetti.

4 **Read and match. Then point, ask and answer.**

a    b   c 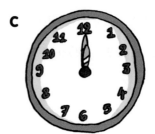   d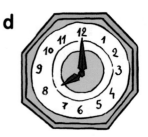

1 It's eight o'clock.   **2** It's twelve o'clock.   **3** It's one o'clock.   **4** It's five o'clock.

What's the time?   It's one o'clock.

The school fair

1 **Listen and number.** •))

 ☐

on

 ☐

under

  ☐

next to

 1

in

2 **Look, read and answer.**

1 How many girls can you see? _five_   **5** Where's the cat? _____
2 How many lions can you see? _____   **6** Where are the frogs? _____
3 How many robots can you see? _____   **7** Where's the clown? _____
4 How many frogs can you see? _____   **8** Where's the teacher? _____

3 **Look at 2. Ask and answer.**

How many frogs can you see?   Ten.

Where's the police officer?   Next to the teacher.

1a He's from Africa.

1 Listen, point and say. 🔊

aunt

uncle

cousin

holiday

airport

Africa

2 Listen and read. 🔊

3 Read again and circle.

1 Ziggy is an elephant / a zebra.

2 He's in Africa / at the airport.

3 He's on holiday / at school.

4 He's from Africa / the zoo.

4 Let's learn! Listen and say. •))

I'm a tiger.
You're an elephant.
He's a zebra.

5 Listen and stick. •))

1 Carlos   **2** Bahar   **3** Anna

6 Look at 5. Read, circle and write.

1 Carlos is from (Argentina) / Poland. His flag is ____blue____ and _____.
2 Bahar is from Turkey / Argentina. Her flag is _____.
3 Anna is from Poland / Turkey. Her flag is _____ and _____.

7 What about you? Write.

I'm from _____ . My flag is _____ .

8 Sing along with the band! •))

I'm from England,
He's from France,
We're from Greece,
Come on, let's dance.
Play and laugh, boys and girls.
You're the children of the world.
Where are you from? Where are you from?
Let's all dance and sing this song.
Where are you from? Where are you from?
Let's all dance and sing this song.

1 Listen, point and say. 🔊

 England
 sauce
 shy
 tired
 hungry

2 Listen and read. 🔊

1 Hello, Ziggy! Welcome to our zoo!

It's nice to meet you.

Thank you. It's nice to meet you, too.

2 This is my aunt and uncle and this is my cousin.

Is she shy?

She's tired.

No, I'm not.

Are you hungry? There's spaghetti with sauce, cheese and ice cream.

3 Are you on holiday?

Yes, we are. England and Turkey!

4 Yes, we are! Thank you, Sa...

3 Read again and write yes or no.

1 Ziggy is at the airport. __no__

2 His cousin is shy. _____

3 Ziggy and his family are on holiday. _____

4 The animals are hungry. _____

4 **Let's learn!** Listen and say. •))

Are you hungry?

No, I'm not.

Is he a monkey? Yes, he is.
Is he shy? No, he isn't.

Are they tired?
Yes, they are.

5 **Look, read and circle.**

1 Is she hungry?
~~Yes she is.~~ /
No, she isn't.

2 Is he tired?
Yes he is. /
No, he isn't.

3 Are they shy?
Yes they are. /
No, they aren't.

4 Are you strong?
Yes I am. /
No, I'm not.

5 Is it big?
Yes it is. /
No, it isn't.

6 Are they happy?
Yes they are. /
No, they aren't.

6 **Play the game.**

zebra
cat
lion
kangaroo
frog
elephant
monkey
tiger

Are you frogs?

Are you kangaroos?

No, we aren't.

Yes, we are.

My e-pals

1 Look at the photos. Find, point and say.

flag   family   tiger   pizza

2 Listen and read. Then number. •))

a ▢

b ▢

c

d

From: Lucy
To: Ewa

Hi!
My name's Lucy. I'm nine. How old are you?
Look at my photos. This is me. (1) My
favourite food is pizza. I like ice cream
too but I don't like cheese. What's your
favourite food?

(2) This is my family – my mum, my dad,
my baby brother and my grandma.

I'm from England. (3) This is my flag.
It's red, white and blue. Where are you
from?

I'm not in England now. I'm on holiday
in France with my mum and dad.
(4) Look, this is the zoo in
Paris. My favourite animals are
tigers. They're beautiful and
strong. I'm happy but I'm shy.
Are you shy?

Write to me soon.
Love
Lucy

3 Read again and write yes or no.

1 Lucy is nine years old. __yes__
2 She's from Argentina. _____
3 She's on holiday in Poland. _____

4 Her favourite animals are zebras. _____
5 Her favourite food is pizza. _____
6 She's shy. _____

4 **Listen and write.** •))

1 Name: _____ *Ewa* _____
2 Age: _____ *9* _____
3 From: _____
4 Colour of flag: _____
5 Favourite food: _____
6 Favourite animal: _____
7 Shy? yes / no

5 **Read and match.**

1 What's your name?
2 How old are you?
3 Where are you from?
4 What's your favourite food?
5 What are your favourite animals?
6 Are you shy?

a No, I'm not.
b Cheese.
c Tigers.
d I'm Tom.
e I'm from France.
f I'm nine.

6 **Ask and write. Use the questions in 5.**

What's your name?

7 **Tell the class.**

He's Adam. He's from Poland. He's ...

15

I've got a camera.

1 **Listen, point and say.** •))

 shorts

 shirt

 map

 camera

 sunglasses

 swimsuit

 smile

2 **Listen and read.** •))

3 **Read again and number in order.**

☐ I've got a new swimsuit.

☐ I've got a camera.

☐ I've got sunglasses and a shirt.

1 You've got lots of clothes.

4 Let's learn! Listen and say. •))

I've got a camera.
She hasn't got a camera.
She's got sunglasses.

We haven't got a camera.
We've got a map.

5 Look and circle.

1 The girl (has got) / hasn't got green shorts.

2 She's got / hasn't got a yellow swimsuit.

3 She's got / hasn't got orange sunglasses.

4 The boy has got / hasn't got black shorts.

5 He's got / hasn't got a blue T-shirt.

6 He's got / hasn't got red shoes.

6 Look at 5 and say.

She's got a white T-shirt.

He hasn't got a white T-shirt.
He's got a blue T-shirt.

7 Sing along with the band! •))

We've got books and bags and pens.
We've got family and we've got friends.
We've got bikes and lots of toys.
We are very lucky girls and boys.
We are very lucky girls and boys.

We've got houses and we've got warm beds.
We've got shoes and hats for our heads.
We've got games and we've got toys.
We are very lucky girls and boys.
We are very lucky girls and boys.

1 Listen, point and say. •))

 plane

 taxi

 passport

 ticket

 money

 suitcase

2 Listen and read. •))

3 Read again and write yes **or** no.

1 The zebras have got their tickets. __yes__
2 They've got their passports. _____
3 Chatter has got their money. _____
4 Sally has got a surprise. _____

4 **Let's learn!** Listen and say. •))

Have you got your camera, Chatter?

Yes, I have.

Has she got a bike?
No, she hasn't.

5 **Listen and tick or cross. Then read and circle.** •))

Sam	✓			
Mary				

1 Has Sam got a mobile phone? Yes, he has. / No, he hasn't.
2 Has Mary got a camera? Yes, she has. / No, she hasn't.
3 Has Sam got a passport? Yes, he has. / No, he hasn't.
4 Has Mary got a computer? Yes, she has. / No, she hasn't.

6 **Look at 5. Ask and answer.**

Has Mary got a mobile phone?

Yes, she has.

7 **Make cards. Then play the game.** page 99

Have you got a camera?

Yes, I have. Here you are.

Hurry up, Harry!

1 Listen, point and say. •))

2 Listen and read. •))

3 Read and match.

1 It's eight o'clock.
2 It's nine o'clock.
3 It's half past two.
4 It's half past three.
5 It's half past nine.

a It's time for bed.
b It's time for football.
c It's time for breakfast.
d It's time for Maths.
e It's time for school.

half past eight

late

hurry up

Maths

cup

5. Hurry up, Harry! It's half past two. It's time for Maths. You're late.

I'm sorry.

6. Hurry up, Sam! It's half past three. It's time for football.

Slow down, Harry!

7. Hooray! We're the winners!

It's four o'clock. Harry is happy!

8. Hurry up, Harry! It's half past nine. It's time for bed.

Look, Mum, I've got the cup! I'm tired. Goodnight.

4 **Choose and write.**

past   cup   late   It   ~~o'clock~~   time   for

It's seven (1) __o'clock__. Harry is in bed. It's time to get up. It's eight o'clock. It's (2) _____ for breakfast. It's half (3) _____ eight. Harry has got his school books. It's nine o'clock. It's time (4) _____ school. It's half past two. Harry is (5) _____ for Maths. (6) _____'s half past three. It's time for football. It's half past nine. It's time for bed. Harry is tired. He's got the (7) _____.

5 **Listen again and act out.** •))

21

Geography

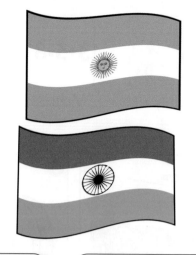

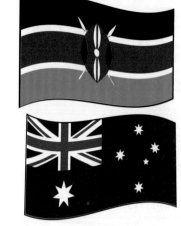

1 Listen, point and read. •))

Where are you from?

a

My name is Kevin. I'm from Australia. I live in the country with my mum and dad. We've got a farm with cows and horses. There are lots of kangaroos here, too.

b

My name is Hasina. I'm from India. I live in Mumbai. It's a very big city. I've got a big family. We live in a very small house.

1

c

My name is Ahadi. I'm from Kenya, in Africa. I live in a small village with my family. It's in a national park. There are lions, zebras and elephants here. I like the elephants.

d

I'm Diego. I'm from Argentina. I live in a flat in Buenos Aires city. It's a big city. I've got two brothers. We like football. Our favourite team is Boca Juniors.

2 Listen and number. •))

3 Read again and circle.

1 Kevin lives in the country. (yes)/ no   **3** Ahadi is from England.   yes / no

2 Hasina has got a big family. yes / no   **4** Diego likes tennis.   yes / no

4 **Choose and write. Then number the photos.**

a

b

c
1

d

Australia ~~India~~ Kenya Argentina farm flat ~~city~~ village

1 Hasina is from ___India___. She lives in a big ___city___. She's got a big family.
2 Ahadi is from _____. She lives in a small _____. She likes the elephants.
3 Diego is from _____. He lives in a _____. He likes football.
4 Kevin is from _____. He lives on a _____. They've got cows and horses.

5 **Say and guess.**

I'm from India.
I live in a big city.
I've got a big family.

You're Hasina.

Right.

6 **Your project!** Where are you from? Write and draw a picture.

My name is Diego.
I'm from Argentina.
I live in a big city.
I've got two brothers.
I like football.

Review 1

1 **What can you see in the picture? Find and circle.**

(suitcase) map spaghetti sunglasses tickets ice cream taxi camera

2 **Listen and number.** •))

3 **Look at 2. Play the game.**

Have you got an ice cream? Yes, I have.

Have you got a suitcase? No, I haven't.

You're 6. Right. My turn.

4 **Listen and chant.** •))

Chicken and chips. Yum, yum!
Jelly and jam. Yum, yum!

5 Play the game.

1 What _____ it?

2 What _____ they?

3 _____ she on holiday?

4 _____ he got a camera?

5 _____ he got a computer game?

6 _____ he excited?

7 _____ he hungry?

8 _____ she _____ a mobile phone?

9 _____ she _____ a book?

10 _____ he _____ a passport?

11 _____ he _____ a suitcase?

12 _____ he _____ sunglasses?

3a He comes every morning.

1 Listen, point and say. •))

 morning   afternoon   evening   postman   postcard   parcel   beach

2 Listen and read. •))

1 Every morning the postman comes at half past seven.

Hello. What have you got today?

There's a postcard for you and a parcel for Sally.

Yippee!

2 The postcard is from Ziggy.

Read it, Karla.

Hello from sunny Turkey. There's a lot to do. In the morning we go to town. In the afternoon we go to the beach. In the evening we play games or watch TV. It's great. Love from Ziggy.

AIR MAIL

Lucky Ziggy!

3 Ooh. A parcel for me.

It isn't your parcel. It's for Sally.

4 Oh, no!

3 Read again and write yes **or** no.

1 There's a parcel for Karla. __no__

2 The postcard is from Ziggy. _____

3 Ziggy is in England. _____

4 Chatter has got the postcard. _____

26

4 Let's learn! Listen and say. •))

I play football. He plays basketball.

We play tennis.

Look!
I go → He goes.
I do → She does.
I have → He has.

5 Listen and stick. Then write. •))

  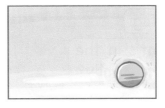 

1 In the morning we ___swim___ .
2 In the afternoon we _____ volleyball.

3 In the evening we _____ TV .
4 At night I _____ .

6 Read and circle.

1 Sally get up / (gets up) at half past six every day.
2 Tag have / has eggs for breakfast every day.
3 Rob and Vicky go / goes to school at half past eight.
4 They do / does their homework in the evening.

7 Sing along with the band! •))

Lucky, lucky Ziggy.
Every day he plays.
Lucky, lucky Ziggy.
He's on holiday.

Lucky, lucky Ziggy.
Every day he plays.
Lucky, lucky Ziggy.
He's on holiday.

He plays on the beach.
He swims in the sea.
He eats an ice cream.
He watches TV.

Do they play basketball?

1 Listen, point and say. •))

 weekend

 year

 winter

 summer

 photo album

 mountain

 ski

2 Listen and read. •))

① Well done, Tag.

What's in the parcel, Sally?

I don't know.

② It's a new photo album.

Look. They're my friends.

Do they play basketball?

No, they don't but they watch it every weekend.

③ This is my family.

Do you ski every year?

Yes, we do. We go to the mountains in winter. We don't go on holiday in summer.

④ Here's a funny photo. Who's this?

It's me!

3 Read again and circle.

1 Sally has got a new photo album / camera.

2 Her friends play / watch basketball.

3 Her family skis every year / weekend.

4 They go on holiday in summer / winter.

4 Let's learn! Listen and say.

He plays basketball.   They don't play basketball.

5 Listen and circle.

1 Yes, I do. /
No, I don't.

2 Yes, we do. /
No, we don't.

3 Yes, they do. /
No, they don't.

4 Yes, I do. /
No, I don't.

6 What about you? Read and circle.

1 Do you go to the beach in summer?   Yes, I do. / No, I don't.
2 Do you watch TV every day?   Yes, I do. / No, I don't.
3 Do you play football every weekend?   Yes, I do. / No, I don't.
4 Do you ski in winter?   Yes, I do. / No, I don't.
5 Do your friends play basketball?   Yes, they do. / No, they don't.

7 Make cards. Then play the game.   page 101

1 **Look at the photos. Find, point and say.**

postcard   mountain   sea   bus   beach   ski

2 **Listen and read. Then number.** •))

1
Dear Sam,
I'm on holiday in France with my family. We go to the beach every morning and swim in the sea. In the afternoon we play football or tennis in the park. It's fun.
Love
Nick

2
Dear Grandma,
We're on holiday in the mountains. In the morning we ski or climb. In the afternoon we go for a walk. In the evening we eat spaghetti or pizza for dinner and then we watch TV. It's great.
Love
Sue

3
Dear John,
I'm on holiday in London. Every day we visit the city. We walk or go by bus. In the afternoon we go to the park or the zoo. I like London.
Love
Jack

3 **Read again and write the name.**

1 He's on holiday in London. ___Jack___
2 She's on holiday in winter. _____
3 He swims in the sea. _____

4 He goes to the city by bus. _____
5 He plays football in the park. _____
6 She watches TV. _____

4 Listen and circle. •))

1 Where do you go on holiday?

A

B

C

2 What do you do in the morning?

A

B

C

3 What do you do in the afternoon?

A

B

C

4 What do you do in the evening?

A

B

C

5 Look at 4. Write and answer.

1 Where __do__ you _____ on holiday?   We _____ .
2 What _____ you _____ in the morning?   I _____ .
3 What _____ you _____ in the afternoon?   I _____ .
4 What _____ you _____ in the evening?   I _____ .

6 Ask and answer about you. Use the questions in 5.

Where do you go on holiday?   I go to the beach.

7 Tell the class.

Alex goes to the beach on holiday.

4a She doesn't like meat.

1 **Listen, point and say.** •))

 panda   China   leaves   meat   awake   excited

2 **Listen and read.** •))

3 **Read again and circle.**

1 Everyone is excited / tired.

2 Pandora is a zebra / a panda.

3 She comes from England / China.

4 She eats leaves / meat.

4 Let's learn! Listen and say. •))

Does he eat meat?
Yes, he does.

Does he eat leaves?
No, he doesn't.

He eats meat.
He doesn't eat leaves.

5 Look, read and circle.

1 Sarah plays / doesn't play tennis.
2 She watches / doesn't watch TV in her bedroom.
3 She likes / doesn't like pandas.

4 Luke plays / doesn't play football.
5 He reads / doesn't read books in his bedroom.
6 He skis / doesn't ski.

6 Look at 5. Ask and answer.

Does Luke play football?   Yes, he does.

7 Sing along with the band! •))

Does Pandora like the zoo?
Yes, she does.
Does she like me and you?
Yes, she does. Yes, she does.
She likes me and you.

Does Chatter like the zoo?
Yes, he does.
Does he like me and you?
Yes, he does. Yes, he does.
He likes me and you.

1 Listen, point and say. •))

bird

show

wake up

want

early

2 Listen and read. •))

1 On Sunday Patty shows Pandora the zoo.

I live here with my family. We live next to the birds. They always wake up early. They never get up late.

2 This is the playground.

Here's Chatter

We sometimes play here in the afternoon.

3 This is Trumpet. He has a shower every day.

4 Oh, dear!

I'm fine. This is fun.

I want a shower, too!

3 **Read again and write** yes **or** no.

1 It's Sunday. __yes__

2 The birds wake up late. _____

3 Trumpet has a shower every day. _____

4 Chatter wants a shower, too. _____

4   Let's learn! Listen and say. •))

- ●   He **always** gets up early.
- ◑   We **sometimes** go to the park.
- ○   They **never** go to school on Sunday.

> I always clean my teeth in the morning.

5   Look and write. Use always, sometimes or never.

always			✓		
sometimes		✓			✓
never	✓			✓	

On Sunday ...

1   John ___never___ wakes up early.
2   He _____ has a shower.
3   He _____ has breakfast.

4   He _____ walks to school.
5   He _____ plays tennis.

6   Write about your Sunday.

1   I _____ get up late in the morning.
2   I _____ go to the park in the afternoon.
3   I _____ do my homework in the evening.

7   Play the game.

walk to school
get up early
eat lunch at school
clean my teeth
go to school on Sunday
go to bed late

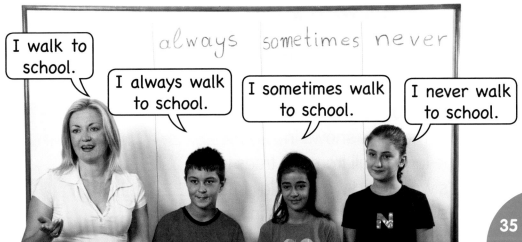

> I walk to school.

> always   sometimes   never

> I always walk to school.

> I sometimes walk to school.

> I never walk to school.

The seasons

Spring

Everyone is happy in spring.
The birds wake up early and sing.
It's warm and we can play
in the park every day.

Summer

In summer it's always hot.
We go to the beach a lot.
In summer it's time to play.
It's a school holiday!

1 Listen, point and say. •))

2 Listen and read. •))

3 Read again and write the season.

1 The birds wake up early and sing in _____spring_____ .

2 We go to the beach a lot in _____ .

3 It sometimes snows in _____ .

4 The leaves fall from the trees in _____ .

5 It's warm and we can play in _____ .

6 It's time for school again in _____ .

spring
 autumn
 snow
 blow
 fall
 warm
 windy

3

Autumn

In autumn we say 'Hello friends'.
It's time for school again.
It's windy and the yellow leaves
fall from the autumn trees.

4

Winter

In winter it sometimes snows.
The days are short, the cold wind blows.
There are no flowers, there are no bees.
There are no leaves on the trees.

4 **Read and match.**

1 Spring is my favourite season because
2 Summer is my favourite season because
3 Autumn is my favourite season because
4 Winter is my favourite season because

a we go to the beach.
b it sometimes snows.
c it's warm and I can play.
d leaves fall from the trees.

5 **Ask and answer.**

What's your favourite season?   My favourite season is winter because it snows.

37

Science

Where do they live?
What do they eat?

1 **Listen, point and read.** 🔊

a

Zebras live on the plains in Africa. It's very hot. Zebras eat grass and leaves. Lots of zebras live and eat together in a herd. ☐

b

Monkeys live in jungles where it's hot and rainy. Monkeys eat fruit, leaves, nuts and flowers. They sometimes eat insects. ☐

c

1

Elephants live in Africa, too. They eat grass, leaves and fruit. Elephants are very big so they eat a lot. They drink water with their long trunks.

d

☐

Penguins live in the snow in Antarctica. They eat fish and small sea animals. Penguins have got wings but they can't fly. They swim in the cold ocean.

e

☐

Pandas live in China. They live in forests in the mountains. It's very rainy. Pandas eat leaves and bamboo. They sometimes eat small animals. They eat a lot every day.

2 **Listen and number.** 🔊

3 **Read again and circle.**

1 Zebras live in jungles. yes / ⦰no⦱ 4 Pandas live on the plains. yes / no
2 Monkeys sometimes eat insects. yes / no 5 Elephants eat grass. yes / no
3 Penguins eat fish. yes / no 6 Monkeys eat bamboo. yes / no

4 **Choose and write.**

snow   ~~forests~~   plains   jungle
grass and leaves   ~~bamboo~~   fruit and nuts   fish

They live in ___forests___ in the mountains.
They eat ___bamboo___ .

2
They live in the _____ .
They eat _____ _____ .

They live on the _____ .
They eat _____ _____ .

4
They live in the _____ in Antarctica.
They eat _____ _____ .

5 **Say and answer.**

They live in the jungle. They eat fruit.
They're monkeys.
Right.

6 **Your project!** Write about an animal. Draw or find a picture.

Pandas live in China.
They live in forests in the mountains.
They eat bamboo and leaves.

Review 2

1 **Choose and write.**

spring   ~~summer~~   autumn   winter

1 In ___summer___ the days are hot.
2 In _____ the leaves fall from the trees.
3 In _____ it sometimes snows.
4 In _____ there are lots of flowers.

2 **Listen and circle.** •))

1 never /

(always)

2 in the afternoon /
in the evening

3 in the morning /
in the evening

4 always /
sometimes

3 **What about you? Write** always, sometimes **or** never. **Then tell the class.**

1 I _____ go to the beach in spring.
2 My family _____ goes on holiday in summer.
3 My friends _____ play tennis in winter.
4 I _____ wear sunglasses in summer.
5 My friends and I _____ play with the leaves in autumn.
6 I _____ wake up early in winter.

4 **Listen and chant.** •))

Vicky plays the violin
every weekend in winter.

5 Play the game.

17

18 ... lions eat fish?

19 He ... go to bed late.

20 FINISH

16 It ... snows in summer.

15 They ... to school in the evening.

14 I like ... because the trees are green.

13

9 Pandas ... eat meat.

10

11 He ... ice cream.

12 She ... at 7 o'clock.

8 ... monkeys eat fruit?

7 Saturday and Sunday are the ...

JU
SATURDAY SUNDAY

6 We ... to the beach in summer.

5 The postman ... in the morning.

1 START

2 ... they ... every winter?

3

4 ... she ... every weekend?

I'm cooking.

1 Listen, point and say. •))

 doorbell
 home
 learn
 cook
 talk
 ring
 bored

2 Listen and read. •))

Tag is playing his guitar. Karla and Trumpet are learning a new song. Chatter is talking to Rob.

1

Hello, Rob. Hello, Vicky. I'm bored.

I've got an idea. Let's visit Sally.

2 Sally is at home.

Hello. I'm cooking. You can help me.

Oh, good.

3 This is fun.

4 Oh, dear. What a mess!

The doorbell is ringing. Who is it?

3 Read again and circle.

1 The animals are / aren't at school.
2 Chatter is bored / excited.

3 Sally is at home / at the beach.
4 The animals help / ring Sally.

4 Let's learn! Listen and say. •))

5 Listen and stick. Then circle. •))

1 My dad is cleaning his teeth.
yes / no

2 My brother is learning the guitar. yes / no

3 My mum is cooking.
yes / no

4 My grandma and grandpa are talking.
yes / no

6 Look at 5. Say and answer.

He's cleaning his teeth.   It's Dad. Picture 1.

7 Sing along with the band! •))

We're cooking in the kitchen.
We are having lots of fun.
We are making a cake
To eat with everyone.

Yum, yum! Yum, yum!
We're eating every crumb!

We're cleaning up the kitchen.
We are having lots of fun.
We are eating the cake.
We're eating every crumb!

43

You aren't helping.

1 **Listen, point and say.** •))

dishes   floor   strawberry   make   wash   taste

2 **Listen and read.** •))

Hello, Sally. Is Chatter here?

Yes, he is. We're making a cake for Tag. It's his birthday. Come in.

Oh, good.

Trumpet, Chatter, you aren't helping.

Yes, we are! I'm washing the dishes.

I'm cleaning the floor. Patty isn't helping.

Yes, I am!

This cake is beautiful.

Trumpet!

I'm not eating the cake. I'm tasting a strawberry.

Hello, Tag! Surprise!

Happy Birthday, Tag!

3 **Read again and write** yes **or** no.

1 They're making a cake for Sally. _no_
2 Chatter is washing the dishes. _____

3 Patty is cleaning the floor. _____
4 Trumpet is tasting a strawberry. _____

4 **Let's learn!** Listen and say. 🔊

I'm not playing basketball.

He isn't playing basketball.

They aren't playing basketball.

5 **Find the differences and write.**

cook   sleep   wash the dishes   ~~clean the floor~~   eat strawberries

1 The man _is cleaning the floor_ .
2 The woman _____ .
3 The girls _____ .
4 The boys _____ .
5 The cat _____ .

1 The man _isn't cleaning the floor_ .
2 The woman _____ .
3 The girls _____ .
4 The boys _____ .
5 The cat _____ .

6 **Make cards. Then play the game.** page 103

I'm washing my hands. Where am I?

No, I'm not.

Yes, I am. Your turn.

park bathroom bedroom
kitchen living room
garden

Are you in the bathroom?

Are you in the kitchen?

5c My birthday party

1 **Look at the photos. Find, point and say.**

cake   hats   presents   candles   friends

2 **Listen and read. Then number.** •))

a

b   1

c

d

1

It's my birthday today. I'm in the kitchen with my mum. She's making my birthday cake. It's got white icing on it! I'm helping my mum. I'm tasting the cake. Mmm! It's lovely.

2

I'm excited! I'm opening my presents in the living room. My sister is helping me. She's excited, too. Wow! I've got a robot, a football, a guitar and a mobile phone.

3

I'm having a birthday party at home. My friends are here. We're wearing party hats. We're dancing and playing party games. We aren't bored. We're all smiling and having lots of fun. I love birthday parties.

4

My friends are singing *Happy Birthday* to me. I'm not singing because I'm blowing out the candles on my cake. There are eight candles. I'm eight today.

3 **Read again and circle.**

1 John is having a birthday party. yes / no

2 His birthday cake has got apples on it. yes / no

3 His friends are singing a song. yes / no

4 He's got lots of presents. yes / no

5 John and his friends are playing football. yes / no

6 They're bored. yes / no

4 Listen and match. •))

Daisy   Peter   Tony

Jane   Anna   Jim

5 Look at 4. Choose and write.

dance   watch   ring   eat   ~~open~~

1 Daisy _____is opening_____ her presents.
2 Peter _____ cake.
3 Tony _____ the doorbell.
4 Jane _____ TV.
5 Anna and Jim _____ .

6 Look at 4. Say and answer.

She's opening her presents.

Right. Your turn.

It's Daisy.

47

Are you going to town?

1 Listen, point and say. •))

supermarket library cinema food rope go shopping buy

2 Listen and read. •))

1
Are you going to town?
Yes, I am. I'm going shopping.
We can help you.
OK.

2
There's the library.
Wow! There's the cinema.
We're going to the supermarket.

3
What are you buying?
Lots of food and a rope. We're making a new swing in the playground.

4
I'm carrying the rope. You can carry the bags. You're strong, Trumpet.
Thank you, Trumpet.

3 **Read again, find and write the name.**

1 I'm going shopping. _Sally_
2 There's the cinema. _____
3 I'm buying food and a rope. _____
4 I'm carrying the rope. _____

4 Let's learn! Listen and say. •))

Is he sitting down?
Yes, he is.
Is he drinking?
No, he isn't.

Are they going
to the library?
No, they aren't.

5 Look and write.

1 __Is__ the man __buying__ (buy) apples?
__No, he isn't.__

2 _____ he _____ (buy) cheese?
_____

3 _____ the woman _____ (stand up)?
_____

4 _____ she _____ (wear) a sweater?
_____

5 _____ they _____ (smile)?
_____

6 Look at 5. Ask and answer.

〔Is he buying rope?〕 〔No, he isn't.〕

spaghetti rope ice cream cheese
sausages strawberries bread eggs

7 Sing along with the band! •))

Are you going to the toy shop?   I'm not going to the toy shop.
Are you going to the zoo?   I'm not going to the zoo.
Are you going to the cinema?   I'm going to the cinema.
Where are you going to?   Are you coming, too?

                                   Yes, I'm coming with you.
                                   Yes, I'm coming with you.

Wait here. Don't move.

1 **Listen, point and say.** •))

 man   thief   wait   move   chase   stop   brave

2 **Listen and read.** •))

① I'm going to the library. Wait here, please. Don't move.

② Look at that man. Why is he running?

Why are the police chasing the man?

You're brave and clever animals. Thank you.

③ Stop, thief!

He's coming this way. Let's help.

④ Well done! Let's go and have an ice cream.

Yummy!

3 **Read again and number in order.**

[ ] The police are chasing the thief.

[ ] The animals are helping the police.

[1] Sally is going to the library.

[ ] The animals have got the thief.

4 Let's learn! Listen and say. •))

5 Listen and circle. •))

1 a b
2 a b
3 a b
4 a b

6 Read and match.

1 Grandma is coming today.
2 This is a library.
3 It's 7 o'clock in the morning.
4 The police are chasing the thief.
5 I'm bored.
6 I'm hungry.

a Let's have lunch.
b Let's go to the cinema.
c Please don't talk.
d Wake up!
e Please don't make a mess.
f Let's help.

7 Play the game.

Sally says 'Dance, please'.

Sally says 'Stop, please'.

Let's sit down.

1. **Listen, point and say.** •))

2. **Listen and read.** •))

3. **Read again and answer.**

1 Are Harry and Adam in the bedroom? _____Yes, they are._____

2 Are they watching TV? _____

3 Is Grandma in the kitchen? _____

4 Is she carrying a saucepan? _____

5 Are the boys playing a computer game? _____

52

saucepan

fight

swing

go for a walk

4️⃣ **Choose and write. Write the correct verb forms.**

fight   ski   watch   swing   mountain   saucepan   ~~bedroom~~

Harry and Adam are in the (1) <u>bedroom</u>. They aren't (2) _____ TV. Adam is
(3) _____ on a rope and Harry is (4) _____ . Now they're climbing a
(5) _____ . Now they're (6) _____ a bear. Grandpa is scared. He's got a
(7) _____ . But there isn't a bear. Harry and Adam are playing a computer game!

5️⃣ **Listen again and act out.** •))

Social Science

What's your job?

1 Listen, point and read. ·))

a

I'm a firefighter. I work at the fire station. I help people in fires. I drive a fire engine. It's very big and it's got lots of water in it.

b

I'm a librarian. I work at the library. I use my computer and help people find books. I read stories to children, too.

c

1
I'm a teacher. I work at the school. I help children with English and Maths.

d

I'm a police officer. I work at the police station. I help people in the town. I usually walk but I sometimes drive a police car.

e

I'm a postwoman. I work at the post office. I get up very early every day. I carry letters and parcels to your home. I don't drive a car, I ride my bike.

2 Listen and number. ·))

3 Read again and circle.

1 She works at the police station. She's a firefighter / police officer.
2 He works at the library. He's a doctor / librarian.
3 He works at the fire station. He's a librarian / firefighter.
4 He works at the school. He's a teacher / police officer.
5 She works at the post office. She's a postwoman / teacher.

4 Listen and number. Then write.

 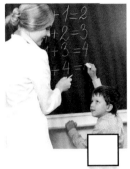   

1 She drives ___a fire engine___ . She's ___a firefighter___ .
2 She teaches children English and _____. She's _____ .
3 He sometimes rides a _____ . He's _____ .
4 She _____ children find books. She's _____ .
5 He sometimes drives a _____ . He's _____ .

5 Play the game.

Do you help children? — Yes I do.
Do you work at the library? — No I don't.
Do you drive a police car? — Yes, I do.
You're a police officer. — Yes, I am.

6 Your project! Write about a job. Draw or find a picture.

This is a police officer. He works at the police station. He helps people. He drives a police car.

This is a zoo keeper. She works at the zoo. She feeds the animals every day and gives them water.

Review 3

1 Choose and write.

librarian   ~~make~~   kitchen   cinema   buy   shop   firefighter   garden

1 cook   learn   jump   _____make_____   _____
2 school   library   supermarket   _____   _____
3 teacher   police officer   postman   _____   _____
4 bathroom   bedroom   living room   _____   _____

2 Listen and circle. Then ask and answer. •))

1 Mum is making a cake / (cooking lunch)
2 Dad is washing the floor / watching TV.
3 Tom is learning the guitar / doing his homework.
4 Susan is talking to mum / reading a book.

> What's Mum doing?
> Is she making a cake?

> No, she isn't.
> She's cooking lunch.

3 What about you? Choose and write. Then tell the class.

learning English   singing   standing up   sitting down
wearing brown shoes   laughing   listening   writing

1 I'm _____ .
2 I'm not _____ .
3 My teacher _____ .
4 We _____ .

4 Listen and chant. •))

She's chasing the shy children to the shop.

5 **Do the quiz.**

START

① She's _____.

② The phone is _____.

③ Are you at home? _____.

④ Are you skiing? _____.

⑤ I'm tasting a _____.

⑥ _____ eat in the classroom.

⑦ Are you wearing black shoes? _____.

⑧ I'm bored. _____ go to the cinema.

⑨ I'm _____ the dishes.

⑩ Help! It's a bear. _____!

⑪ They're _____ basketball.

⑫ Wait here, please. Don't _____!

⑬ Are they reading? _____.

⑭ Is she buying a rope? _____.

⑮ It's my birthday. Let's _____ a cake.

⑯ The kitchen is a mess. _____ clean the floor.

⑰ Is she going to the cinema? _____.

⑱ He's _____ the thief.

⑲ This is a library. Please _____ talk.

⑳ I _____ learning English.

WELL DONE!

FINISH

These are crabs.

1 **Listen, point and say.** •))

fish   crab   dolphin   turtle   take a photo   rain

2 **Listen and read.** •))

1. Oh, no! It's raining.
I've got a good idea. Let's go and see the fish.

2. What's this?
It's a dolphin. And that's a turtle.

3. What are these?
They're crabs. Look, these are fish. They're my favourites!

4. You've got your camera. Can you take a photo of me, please?
Yes, of course.
Oh, dear!

3 **Read again and write** yes **or** no.

1. It's sunny. __no__
2. Patty and Tag are looking at the fish. _____
3. Patty has got her camera. _____
4. There's a crab in the photo. _____

4 Let's learn! Listen and say. •))

This is an octopus.

These are crabs.

5 Listen and stick. Then match and write This is or These are. •))

1   2   3   4

a _____   b _____   c _These are_   d _____
fish.   a dolphin.   crabs.   a turtle.

6 Look at 5. Point, ask and answer.

What are these?   These are fish.   What's this?   This is a turtle.

7 Sing along with the band! •))

This is a fish.
It's swimming in the sea.
I can see the fish
and it can see me.
It can see me.

These are dolphins.
They're swimming in the sea.
I can see the dolphins
and they can see me.
They can see me.

It's got big teeth.

1 **Listen, point and say.** •))

 people

 men

 women

 teeth

 shark

 feed

 tall

2 **Listen and read.** •))

① Lots of people are at the pool. Two men are feeding the sharks.

I can't see. These women are very tall.

Come here, Patty!

② Wow! Look at this shark! Look at its teeth! Patty, where are you?

③ I'm here.

Patty, there's a big shark in the pool.

It's OK. The shark is my friend!

3 **Read again and circle.**

1 The men are eating / feeding the sharks.
2 The women / men are tall.
3 The shark has got big teeth / feet.
4 The shark is in the park / pool.

4 Let's learn! Listen and say. •))

watch	watches	strawberry	strawberries	foot	feet
fox	foxes	baby	babies	child	children
dress	dresses	family	families	man	men
dish	dishes	spy	spies	woman	women
				fish	fish

5 Choose and write.

baby   fox   woman   ~~child~~   man

1 The ___children___ are on the swings.

2 The _____ are sleeping.

3 The _____ are reading.

4 The _____ are playing tennis.

5 The _____ are hiding.

6 Look at 5. Ask and answer.

What are the children doing?   They're playing on the swings.

Right.

7 Make cards. Then play the game. page 105

These are babies.
Look, 'babies'. It's
a pair.

The aquarium

1 Look at the photos. Find, point and say.

shark   fish   turtle   children   dolphin

2 Listen and read. Then number. •))

WELCOME TO
THE BLUE SEA AQUARIUM

Come and visit the Blue Sea Aquarium. It's a great day out for families. We open at 8 o'clock every morning so come early and have fun. Look at these photos of our sea animals.

1 These fish are hungry! The children are feeding them.
2 These are clownfish. They're beautiful colours – yellow, orange, black and white. Lots of people have got clownfish at home as pets.
3 These people are brave. They're walking next to the sharks. The sharks have got lots of big teeth. Don't worry. Sharks don't eat people. They eat fish and crabs.
4 There's a dolphin show every day at the aquarium. Look at these dolphins. They're jumping and playing.
5 This is a green turtle. It's very big. It hasn't got feet. It's got flippers for swimming.

3 Read again and circle.

1 The children are feeding the fish / turtle.
2 Sharks eat people / crabs.
3 The green turtle has got feet / flippers.
4 The clownfish are orange and white / pink and green.
5 The dolphins are jumping / sleeping.

4 **Listen and draw the route. Then write.** •))

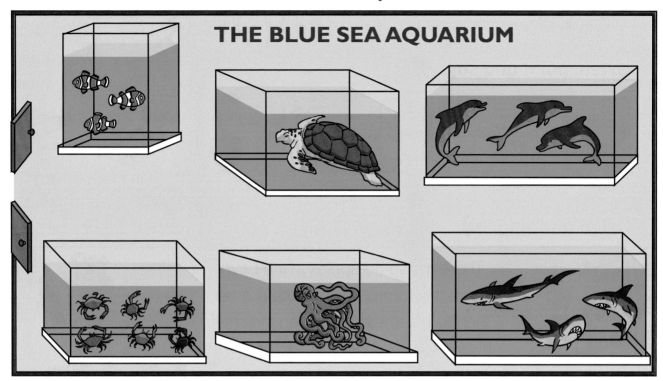

THE BLUE SEA AQUARIUM

The children don't visit the _____ .

5 **Listen again and match.** •))

1 Look at these fish.

2 This is a turtle.

3 This is an octopus.

4 Look at these sharks.

5 These are dolphins.

a They've got very big teeth.

b They're my favourites.

c Look at its flippers.

d They're beautiful colours.

e It's got lots of arms.

6 **Look, point and say.**

These are sharks. They're grey.

These are dolphins. They can jump.

These are sharks.

This is an octopus.

These are dolphins.

This is a turtle.

These are fish.

This is a whale.

This is a crab.

1 Listen, point and say.

bowl   shelf   drawer   carrot   cherry   sweets   chocolates

2 Listen and sing.

There are some apples in the bowl.
There are some carrots in the drawer.
There are some bananas on the shelf.
But we're looking for the **Secret Store**!

Are there any cherries?
Are there any sweets?
Are there any chocolates?
Are there any treats?

There aren't any cherries in the bowl.
There aren't any sweets in the drawer.
There aren't any chocolates on the shelf.
But here it is, the **Secret Store**!

There are lots of cherries.
There are lots of sweets.
There are lots of chocolates.
There are lots of treats.

3 Read again and match.

1 The apples are
2 The carrots are
3 The bananas are

a on the shelf.
b in the bowl.
c in the drawer.

4 Let's learn! Listen and say. •))

Are there any apples?
Yes, there are.

Are there any cherries?
No, there aren't.

There are some bananas.
There aren't any cherries.

5 Write some or any. Then match.

1 There are __some__ apples in the bowl. There aren't _____ bananas. __A__
2 There are _____ photos on the shelf. There aren't _____ books. _____
3 There are _____ flowers under the shelf. There aren't _____ carrots. _____
4 There are _____ sweets on the table. There aren't _____ cakes. _____
5 There are _____ school bags on the door. There aren't _____ clothes. _____
6 There are _____ people next to the window. There aren't _____ trees. _____

6 Make cards. Then play the game. page 107

Are there any chairs in our classroom?

Yes, there are.

Is there any pizza?

1 Listen, point and say. •))

fridge

butter

water

omelette

fruit salad

2 Listen and read. •))

What are you doing? Why are you eating the sweets?

Sorry, Sally. We're hungry.

It's time for lunch. Is there any pizza in the fridge?

There's some milk and some butter.

There's some water. But there isn't any pizza.

Is there any cheese?

Yes, there's lots of cheese.

Are there any eggs?

Yes, there are.

Good, I've got an idea. Let's make a cheese omelette.

We can make a fruit salad, too. We've got apples and bananas.

3 **Read again and write** yes **or** no.

1 The animals are hungry. __yes__   **3** There are some eggs in the fridge. _____

2 It's time for breakfast. _____   **4** Patty wants to make a cake. _____

4 **Let's learn!** Listen and say. •))

5 Listen and stick. Then write. •))

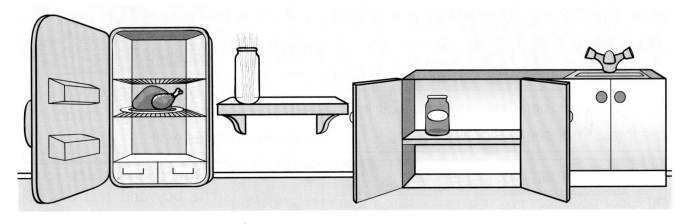

1 In the fridge there's some ___butter___ and some _____ .
2 On the shelf there's some _____ .
3 In the cupboard there's some _____ .

6 **Look at 5. Ask and answer.**

ice cream   cheese   chicken   butter
milk   fruit   water   spaghetti
jelly   honey   salad   bread

Is there any ice cream in the fridge?
Yes, there is.
Is there any cheese in the cupboard?
No, there isn't.

7 **Play the game.**

In my fridge I've got some ice cream and some cheese.

In my fridge I've got some ice cream.

In my fridge I've got some ice cream, some cheese and some butter.

① Look at that house, Greta.

Harry and his sister, Greta, go for a walk in the forest. They see a beautiful house.

② There are sweets and cakes on the doors and windows. There are biscuits and chocolates on the walls.

A very old woman lives in the house.

③ Good morning. I've got some cakes and sweets in my house. Please come in.

Thank you.

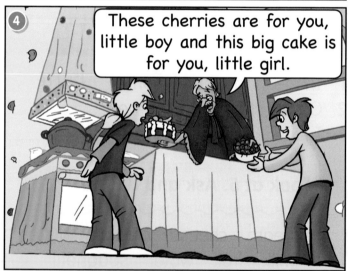

④ These cherries are for you, little boy and this big cake is for you, little girl.

1 Listen, point and say. •))

2 Listen and read. •))

3 Read again and answer.

1 Where's the house? _____It's in the forest._____

2 What's on the walls? _____

3 What has the old woman got for Harry? _____

4 What can Greta see in the trees? _____

5 What do the squirrels eat? _____

6 Is the old woman happy? _____

biscuit

wall

squirrel

little

angry

(5) Aha! Now I've got you! Get in the cupboard!

Help!

Greta can see some squirrels in the trees.

(6) Please, come and help my brother!

The squirrels eat the biscuits and chocolates. They eat the walls and the doors! Greta opens the cupboard.

(7) Stop it! You're eating my house!

Greta and Harry run away. They're happy. The old woman is very angry.

(8) Thank you, squirrels!

4 **Choose and write.**

biscuits   angry   walls   little   squirrels   ~~forest~~

Harry and his sister, Greta see a house in the (1) _____forest_____ . There are (2) _____ and chocolates on the (3) _____ . They meet an old woman. She's got cherries for Harry and a cake for Greta. She puts the (4) _____ boy in a cupboard. Greta asks the (5) _____ to help her brother. They eat the doors, windows and walls of the house. Greta and Harry run away. The old woman is very (6) _____ .

5 **Listen again. Now you tell the story.** •))

69

Science

Do you eat a healthy diet?

1 Listen, point and read. •))

The 'eat well' plate

Fruit and vegetables

Bread, rice, potatoes and pasta

Milk, cheese, butter and yoghurt

Meat, fish and eggs

Biscuits, sweets, chocolates and crisps

Bread, rice, potatoes and pasta are good for you. They give you energy and help you work well at school. Eat these with every meal.

Meat, fish and eggs help your body grow big. But don't eat lots of red meat because it's got lots of fat. Eat two portions of fish every week.

Fruit and vegetables keep you healthy. Eat five portions every day. You can eat a banana with breakfast, salad with lunch, an apple in the afternoon and carrots and peas with dinner.

Milk, cheese, butter and yoghurt make your bones strong. But don't eat lots of cheese or butter because they've got lots of fat. Eat two portions of cheese every week.

2 Listen and number. •))

Biscuits, sweets, cakes, chocolates and crisps aren't good for you. They've got lots of sugar, fat and salt. You can eat these sometimes as a treat but don't eat lots.

3 Read again and write.

1 Bread, rice and pasta give you ___energy___ .
2 Eat five _____ of fruit and vegetables every day.
3 Red meat has got lots of _____ .
4 Milk, cheese and yoghurt make your _____ strong.
5 Sweets and crisps have got lots of fat, _____ and _____ .

4 **Read and tick or cross.**

1 Eat bread, rice or pasta with every meal. ✓
2 Eat fruit and vegetables every day. _____
3 Eat red meat for dinner every day. _____
4 Eat lots of butter and cheese. _____
5 Eat chocolate as a special treat. _____
6 Eat lots of sugar and salt. _____

✓	healthy
✗	not healthy

5 **Do you eat a healthy diet? Tick or cross. Then ask and answer.**

I eat these foods …						
with every meal						
every day						
every week						
sometimes						
as a treat						

How often do you eat potatoes or pasta?

With every meal.

Good. That's healthy.

6 **Your project!** Make an 'eat well' plate.

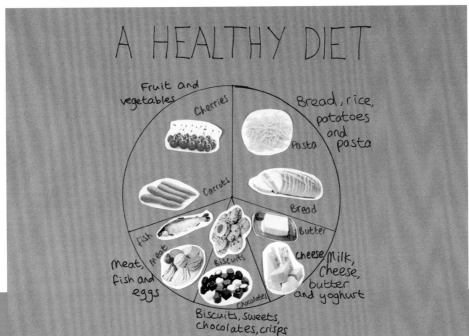

A HEALTHY DIET

Fruit and vegetables
Cherries
Carrots
fish
meat, fish and eggs
meat
Biscuits
Chocolates
Biscuits, sweets, chocolates, crisps
cheese
Milk, cheese, butter and yoghurt
Butter
Bread
Pasta
Bread, rice, potatoes and pasta

Review 4

1 **Find the odd one out. Then write.**

1	apples	(sharks)	cherries	bananas
2	crabs	men	women	children
3	cakes	biscuits	chocolates	dolphins
4	omelette	butter	turtles	water
5	fish	teeth	hair	feet

You can see (1) ___sharks___ ,
(2) _____ ,
(3) _____ ,
(4) _____ and
(5) _____ in the sea.

2 **What's in the fridge? Listen and tick or cross.** •))

3 **Look at 2. Ask and answer.**

Is there any butter in the fridge?   Yes, there is.

Are there any cherries?   No, there aren't.

4 **Listen and chant.** •))

Three girls with thirteen purple turtles.

72

5 **Play the game.**

1 How many _____ are there?

2 How many _____ are there?

3 How many _____ are there?

4 How many _____ are there?

5 What's this?
_____

6 What are these?
_____

7 Is there _____ bread on the table?

8 Are there _____ carrots in the bag?

9 _____ there _____ biscuits in the bowl?

10 _____ there _____ butter on the dish?

11 _____ there _____ birds in the trees?

12 _____ there _____ crabs in the water?

1 Listen, point and say. ◀))

 accident

 nurse

 finger

 cry

 middle

2 Listen and read. ◀))

① Vicky is at the hospital. She's crying.

Quick. Where's the nurse?

Here I am.

What's the matter?

② We were in the playground. Chatter was on his rollerblades and Tag was on his bike and there was an accident.

And I was in the middle. Look at my fingers.

③ You were lucky. Everything is OK. Karla, please go home with Vicky.

3 Choose and write.

fingers   nurse   ~~crying~~   home

1 Vicky is ___crying___ .

2 Her _____ aren't OK.

3 The _____ is helping Vicky.

4 Vicky and Karla are going _____ .

4 Let's learn! Listen and say. •))

> On Saturday I was in the playground.
> On Sunday we were at the beach.

Saturday   Sunday   Monday

5 Look and write was or were.

On Sunday it (1) _____was_____ hot
and sunny. I (2) _____ with
my dad and my baby brother.
We (3) _____ at the park.
The trees (4) _____ green.
My brother (5) _____ tired.
I (6) _____ happy.
The ducks (7) _____ hungry.

6 Write about you. Then tell the class.

1 On Saturday I _____ .
2 On Sunday I _____ .
3 My friends _____ .

> at home
> at the shops / park
> in the garden / playground
> with my mum / grandpa

7 Sing along with the band! •))

It was a hot afternoon.
I was at the zoo.
I was at the zoo.

I was with all of my friends.
Tag and Chatter were there, too.
Tag and Chatter were there, too.

Chatter was on his rollerblades.
Tag was on his bike.
Tag was on his bike.

There was an accident
in the playground.
But we are all right.
But we are all right.

I wasn't careful.

1 **Listen, point and say.** •))

 bandage ambulance  grapes yesterday

2 **Listen and read.** •))

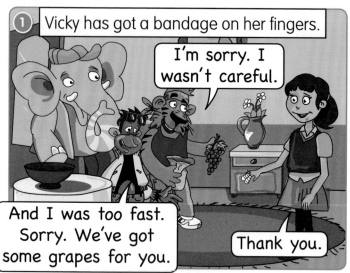

1 Vicky has got a bandage on her fingers.
I'm sorry. I wasn't careful.
And I was too fast. Sorry. We've got some grapes for you.
Thank you.

2 Were you in an ambulance?
No, I wasn't.

3 Were you and Chatter OK yesterday?
Yes, we were. And my bike was OK, too.

4 Where are the grapes?
Trumpet!
Sorry, Vicky. I can get you some more.

3 **Read again and write** yes **or** no.

1 Vicky was in an accident. __yes__
2 She's got a bandage on her head. _____

3 Tag and Chatter are sorry. _____
4 They've got some grapes for Vicky. _____

76

4 Let's learn! Listen and say. •))

Were you scared yesterday?

Yes, I was.

She was scared.
She wasn't happy.

Were you at the hospital yesterday?

No, we weren't.

They weren't at the hospital.
They were at the zoo.

5 Listen and match. Then write. Use was/wasn't or were/weren't. •))

1 Anna   **2** Alex   **3** Carol and Sue   **4** Tom and Pete

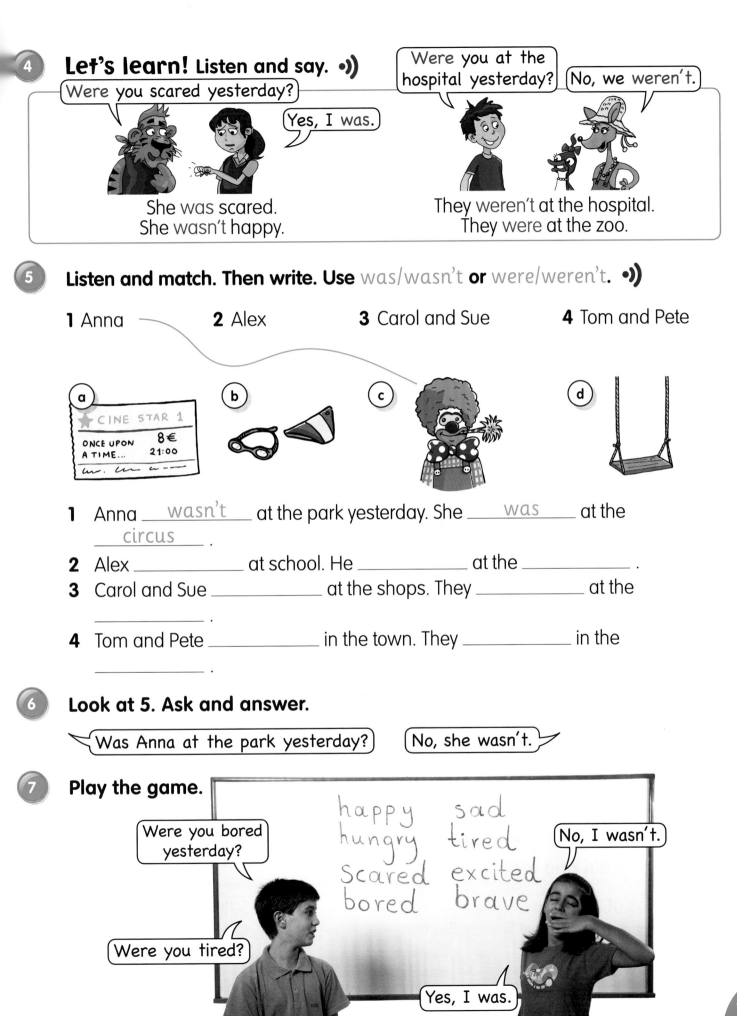

a   CINE STAR 1   ONCE UPON A TIME...   8€   21:00

b

c

d

1 Anna ___wasn't___ at the park yesterday. She ___was___ at the ___circus___ .

2 Alex _____ at school. He _____ at the _____ .

3 Carol and Sue _____ at the shops. They _____ at the _____ .

4 Tom and Pete _____ in the town. They _____ in the _____ .

6 Look at 5. Ask and answer.

Was Anna at the park yesterday?

No, she wasn't.

7 Play the game.

Were you bored yesterday?

No, I wasn't.

happy   sad
hungry   tired
Scared   excited
bored   brave

Were you tired?

Yes, I was.

Last weekend

1 **Look at the photos. Find, point and say.**

clown   robot   hospital   cinema

2 **Listen and read. Then number.** •))

> Last weekend I was very busy.

Ben

SATURDAY

At ten o'clock in the morning I was in town with my friends. We were in the toy shop. The robots were great but my favourites were the cars.
At two o'clock in the afternoon I was at the cinema with my sister. The film was about ghosts. I wasn't scared but my sister was scared.

SUNDAY

At eleven o'clock in the morning I was at the hospital. My cousin was there because he was in an accident last week. He's OK but he's got a bandage on his leg. The nurses were very nice.
At half past three in the afternoon I was at the circus with my friends. The horses were beautiful. The clowns were very funny. The acrobats were my favourites. They were very good. It was a great weekend.

a

b
1

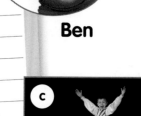
c

d

3 **Read again and match.**

1 Ben was at the circus	**a** on Saturday morning.
2 He was at the hospital	**b** on Saturday afternoon.
3 He was in town	**c** on Sunday morning.
4 He was at the cinema	**d** on Sunday afternoon.

4 Listen and match. Then write. •))

1

2

3

Where was Daisy?

Monday

Tuesday

Wednesday

Thursday

Friday

Saturday

Sunday

4

5

6

Daisy was at home on _____.

5 Look at 4. Choose and write.

park   zoo   beach   home   shops   cinema   library

My Diary by Daisy

Monday
at the ___library___

Tuesday
at the _____

Wednesday
at the _____

Thursday
at the _____

Friday
at the _____

Saturday
at the _____

Sunday
at _____

6 Look at 5. Ask and answer.

Where was Daisy last Saturday?

She was at the beach.

1 Listen, point and say.

boat

museum

statue

sail

stay

2 Listen and read.

Hi Sally!
I'm having a fantastic holiday in Turkey! Last weekend was great. I was very busy. On Saturday I sailed on a boat. It was wet and windy, but I wasn't scared.

On Sunday we climbed a mountain. It was very high. After that we were all tired. In the evening we stayed at home and watched TV.

This morning we visited a museum. I liked the statues.

I've got an idea! Why don't you come to Turkey and have a holiday, too?

3 Read again and write.

1 Last __weekend__ Ziggy was on a boat.
2 On _____ he was in the mountains.

3 In the _____ he was at home.
4 This _____ he was at a museum.

4 Let's learn! Listen and say. •))

Yesterday I played basketball.

Monday	
Tuesday	Today
Wednesday	
Thursday	
Friday	
Saturday	
Sunday	

cleaned   helped   visited
climbed   jumped   waited
listened   talked
played   watched
sailed   walked   **Look!**
stayed   washed   liked

5 Look, read and circle.

1    **2**    **3**    **4**

Last Saturday Harry was very busy. In the morning he (cleaned) / climbed his bedroom.
Then he played / helped his dad. They watched / washed the car. In the afternoon he
visited / helped his aunt and uncle. After that he watched TV / played football.

6 What about you? Circle. Then tell the class.

watched TV   helped my mum   played volleyball
listened to music   visited my grandma
cleaned my bedroom   played with my friends

Last Saturday I ...

7 Sing along with the band! •))

Yesterday I walked to school
and I talked to all my friends.
Yesterday I was at school
and I played with all my friends.

We climbed, we jumped, we played basketball.
We liked our day at our lovely school!

Yesterday I walked to school
and I laughed with all my friends.
Yesterday I was at school.
I was happy with my friends.

Did he sail on a boat?

1 **Listen, point and say.** •))

 email
 wave
 dive
 surf
 row
 phone

2 **Listen and read.** •))

1 Sally has got an email from Ziggy.
Please read it to us, Sally!
Listen! 'Last weekend I was very busy ...'

2 What did he do? Did he dive in the sea?
Did he surf on the waves?
No, he didn't.

3 Did he row a boat on the sea?
He didn't row a boat. He sailed on a boat.
Lucky Ziggy!

4 Listen! We can visit Ziggy and have a holiday, too.
Great! Let's phone Rob and Vicky! Let's all go to Turkey.

3 **Read and circle.**

1 Sally has got a postcard from Ziggy. yes / no
2 Ziggy surfed on the waves. yes / no
3 Ziggy sailed on a boat last week. yes / no
4 The animals are excited. yes / no

4 **Let's learn!** Listen and say. •))

Did you dive in the sea yesterday?

Did you climb a mountain?

Yes, I did.

No, I didn't.

He dived in the sea.
He didn't climb a mountain.

5 Listen and tick or cross. Then circle. •))

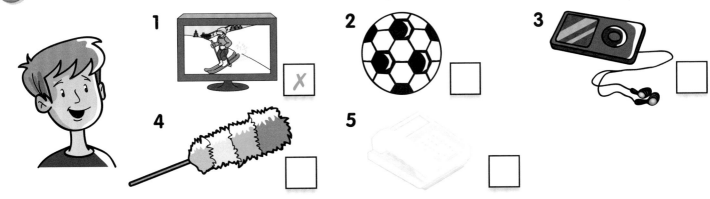

1 ✗

2

3

4

5

1 Did Jack watch TV yesterday?	Yes, he did. /	No, he didn't.
2 Did he play football?	Yes, he did. /	No, he didn't.
3 Did he listen to music?	Yes, he did. /	No, he didn't.
4 Did he clean his bedroom?	Yes, he did. /	No, he didn't.
5 Did he phone his friend?	Yes, he did. /	No, he didn't.

6 **Look at 5. Ask and answer.**

Did Jack watch TV yesterday?

No, he didn't.

7 **Make cards. Then play the game.** page 109

Did you watch TV yesterday?

Did you phone your grandma yesterday?

Yes, I did.

No, I didn't.

Last summer Sam and Katie were on holiday in England. They visited London for a week.

On the first day they visited Buckingham Palace. The Queen wasn't at home.

On the second day they visited Hyde Park. It was a sunny day. Sam and Katie rowed a boat on the Serpentine Lake. It was fun.

On the third day they were at the Houses of Parliament. They listened to Big Ben. It was 8 o'clock.

1 **Listen, point and say.** •))

2 **Listen and read.** •))

3 **Read again and write** yes **or** no.

1 Sam and Katie visited London last summer. __yes__
2 They talked to the Queen. _____
3 They dived in the Serpentine Lake. _____
4 They liked the dinosaurs in the museum. _____
5 They were scared on the London Eye. _____
6 They visited Madame Tussaud's on the last day. _____

first second third fourth fifth  sixth last

On the fourth day it rained. They visited the Natural History Museum. They liked the dinosaurs. They were scared!

On the fifth day they were on the London Eye next to the River Thames. It was very high. They weren't scared. They were excited.

On the sixth day they visited Madame Tussaud's Museum. There were lots of famous people. Prince William was their favourite.

On the last day they visited lots of shops in Oxford Street. They were very happy. It was a great holiday.

4 **Choose and write.**

last   were   ~~visited~~   first   fourth   Museum   Big Ben

Sam and Katie were on holiday last summer. They (1) _visited_ London. On the (2) _____ day they visited Buckingham Palace. On the second day they visited Hyde Park. On the third day they listened to (3) _____. On the (4) _____ day they visited the Natural History Museum. On the fifth day they (5) _____ on the London Eye. On the sixth day they visited Madame Tussaud's (6) _____. On the (7) _____ day they were in Oxford Street.

5 **Listen again. Now you tell the story.** •))

How can you take care of your body?

1 Listen, point and read. •))

a
Be careful. Don't run too fast in the playground.

I'm at the hospital. I've got a bandage on my arm. There was an accident in the playground. The nurse is showing me an X-ray. My arm is broken.

b
You need glasses to help you see.

I can't see the board when I sit at the back of the classroom. I'm visiting the optician. He's looking at my eyes.

c
Don't eat lots of sweets. Clean your teeth after meals.

I'm visiting the dentist because I've got toothache. My teeth hurt when I eat hot food or when I drink cold drinks.

d
You've got a cold. Take this medicine every morning and night. Stay in bed. Drink lots of water.

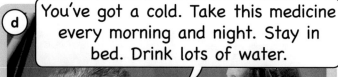

I'm visiting the doctor because I've got a cough and I've got a temperature. I'm sneezing a lot, too.

2 Listen and number. •))

3 Read again and write.

1 A __dentist__ helps me when I've got toothache.

2 A _____ gives me medicine when I'm not well.

3 An _____ looks at my eyes and gives me glasses.

4 A _____ looks after me when I'm in hospital.

4 **Choose and write. Then listen and match.** •))

cold ~~broken~~ toothache see

1 My finger is ___broken___ .

2 I've got a bad _____ .

3 I've got _____ .

4 I can't _____ the board very well.

a You need glasses. Go to the optician.

b Always be careful in the playground. Don't run too fast.

c Stay in bed. Use a tissue when you sneeze.

d Go to the dentist every six months. Always clean your teeth after meals.

5 **Say and answer.**

I've got a cold.   Stay in bed.

6 **Your project!** **Draw and write about how to take care of your body.**

Don't get a cold. Eat lots of fruit and drink lots of water. Use a tissue when you sneeze.

Take care of your teeth. Don't eat lots of sweets. Clean your teeth after meals. Go to the dentist every six months.

Review 5

1 Listen and say the name.

Monday   Tuesday

(Yes, I did.) (No, I didn't.)   (Yes, I did.) (No, I didn't.)

Wednesday   Thursday   Friday

(Yes, I did.) (No, I didn't.)   (Yes, I did.) (No, I didn't.)   (Yes, I did.) (No, I didn't.)

James   Lucy   Tom   Mary

2 Look at 1. Ask and answer.

- Did you watch TV on Monday? — Yes, I did.
- Did you play tennis on Wednesday? — No, I didn't.
- You're Lucy. — Yes, that's right.

3 Listen and chant.

The cowboy and clown were in town.

4 Play the game.

17

18 Did you … your teeth this morning?

19 They … listen to the radio last night.

20 FINISH

16 … they at the cinema yesterday?

15 He … his bedroom this morning.

14 We … at the zoo yesterday.

13

9 He wasn't first. He was … .

10

11 I … at a museum last weekend.

12 Did she … on the waves?

8 Today it's Monday. Yesterday was … .

YESTERDAY TODAY MONDAY T

7 He was scared. He … brave.

6 Did you … on a boat last week?

5 She … play tennis this morning.

1 START

2 I … at the cinema on Saturday.

CINEMA

3

4 Did she watch TV yesterday?

We want to visit Ziggy.

1 Listen, point and say. 🔊

 flippers

 snorkel

 towel

 video camera

 pack

 take

 ready

2 Listen and read. 🔊

① Everyone is excited. They want to go on holiday.

Hi, Rob. Hi, Vicky. Do you want to go to Turkey with us?

Yes, we do. We want to visit Ziggy!

Yippee! I can't wait!

② I want to dive in the sea.

I want to surf in the waves.

Hurry! Go and pack your suitcases.

③ The animals are packing.

We've got our flippers, snorkels, swimsuits and towels.

We want to take the video camera.

④ Are you ready, everyone?

Yes, we're ready.

Come on, let's go!

3 Read again and circle.

1 Patty is taking (flippers) a bandage a swimsuit a towel a passport.
2 Karla is taking shorts sunglasses a map a video camera a photo album.
3 Rob is taking sunglasses a map a hat a radio flippers.

4 Let's learn! Listen and say. •))

Do you want to play football tomorrow?

Monday
Tuesday
Wednesday
Thursday
Friday — Today
Saturday — Tomorrow
Sunday

No, I want to go swimming.

Tag wants to go swimming.
He doesn't want to play football.

5 Listen and circle. •))

What do they want to do tomorrow?
1 Tom wants to play football / play basketball.
2 Daisy wants to go shopping / go swimming.
3 Mary wants to go to the aquarium / go to the zoo.
4 Sam wants to go the beach / go to the mountains.

6 What about you? Ask and answer.

go for a walk   play volleyball   go swimming   fly a kite   visit my friends
go to the cinema   go to the zoo   play computer games

Do you want to go for a walk tomorrow?   **No, I don't.**

Do you want to go to the cinema?   **Yes, I do.**

7 Sing along with the band! •))

I want to go to the beach.
I want to swim in the sea.
I want to play with my friends.
Do you want to come with me?

Yes, please! Yes, please!
I want to go on holiday.
Yes, please! Yes, please!
I want to play all day.

Do you want to go on holiday?
Do you want to swim in the sea?
Do you want to see some fish?
Do you want to come with me?

11b

Can we make a sandcastle?

1 Listen, point and say. •))

 armbands
 sandcastle
 bucket
 spade
 sun cream
 use

2 Listen and read. •))

1. Sally and the animals go to the beach.

Welcome to Turkey!

Hello, Ziggy!

2. I've got my armbands on. Can we go in the sea?

Yes, you can.

Can I have an ice cream?

No, you can't. Not now.

3. Can we make a sandcastle? We've got our buckets and spades.

You can make a sandcastle under the umbrella. The sun is very hot.

4. You're pink and black!

I know! I haven't got my sun cream.

You can use our sun cream. Here you are.

Thank you.

3 Read again. Find and write.

armbands   buckets   ~~beach~~   sun cream

1 Sally and the animals are at the __beach__ .

2 Karla is wearing her _____ .

3 Trumpet and Tag have got their _____ and spades.

4 Ziggy hasn't got his _____ .

4 **Let's learn!** Listen and say. •))

5 Listen and tick or cross. •))

1  ☒

2

3

4

6 **Look at 5. Write** Yes, he/she/they can **or** No, he/she/they can't.

1 Can she have an ice cream? _____
2 Can they watch TV? _____
3 Can he use her camera? _____
4 Can they swim in the sea? _____

7 **Read and tick or cross. Then ask and answer.**

Can you ...	You	Your friend
watch TV in your bedroom?	___	___
get up late on Saturday?	___	___
go to bed late on Saturday?	___	___
play football in your living room?	___	___
eat chocolates for breakfast?	___	___
climb trees in the garden?	___	___
sleep at your friend's house?	___	___
use a mobile phone at school?	___	___

11c A fantastic holiday!

1 **Look at the photos. Find, point and say.**

flippers   friends   mountains   tent   fire

2 **Listen and read. Then number.** •))

CAMP FUN!

ACTIVITY HOLIDAYS FOR YOU

Do you want to have a fantastic holiday? Do you want to make new friends? Do you want to learn something new? Come to one of our great holiday camps!

a

b

c

WATER FUN

1 Do you love watersports? At Water Fun you can swim in the sea and surf in the waves. Or you can swim in the pool in our fantastic sports centre. You can learn to dive and sail a boat. Remember to pack your swimsuit and flippers – and lots of sun cream.

CAMPING FUN

2 Do you love camping? At Camping Fun you can sleep in a tent. You can go for a walk in the country or you can ride a bike. You can cook your food on a fire.

MOUNTAIN FUN

3 Do you love the mountains? At Mountain Fun you can walk and climb in the mountains. In autumn you can see bears and other animals – be careful! In winter you can ski. Remember to bring warm clothes and boots. You can buy skis at the Camp.

3 **Read again and circle.**

1 At Water Fun you can surf in the waves / climb a mountain.
2 At Camping Fun you can ski / sleep in a tent.
3 At Mountain Fun you can see bears / swim in the sea.

4 **Answer for you.**

1 Where do you want to go? To _____ .
2 Why? Because I want to _____ .

5 Listen and match. •))

1 Tom and Paul   **2** Jane and Anna   **3** Sue and Peter   **4** Alex and Sally

  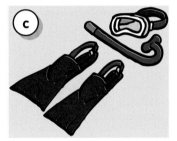 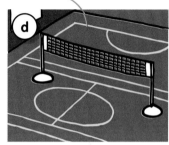

a   b   c   d

6 Number in order. Then listen and say. •))

Hello, Sue. | 1

Good idea. I've got my swimsuit. | ☐

No, not today. It's too cold. | ☐

Me too. Let's go. | ☐

Yes, you're right. Do you want to go to the swimming pool? | ☐

Hello, Peter. Do you want to swim in the sea today? | ☐

7 Ask and answer.

Do you want to go swimming?

Good idea. Let's go to the swimming pool.

go for a walk
go shopping
play basketball
see the fish
go swimming
play computer games

the aquarium
the swimming pool
my house
the sports centre
the country
the town

95

You must be brave.

1 **Listen, point and say.** 🔊

| monster | net | far | near | stuck | worried |

2 **Listen and read.** 🔊

1 Sally is worried. Patty isn't wearing armbands.

Look, Sally. I'm swimming.

Patty! You mustn't swim far. You must stay near the beach.

2 Patty is scared.

Help!   What's the matter, Patty?

There's a monster in the sea!

3 I'm not a monster! I'm a turtle. I'm Carrie Caretta. I can't move.

Carrie Caretta is stuck in a net.

4 You must be brave, Carrie. You mustn't cry.

We must help Carrie.

Everyone wants to help Carrie.

3 **Read again and circle.**

1 Sally /(Patty) is swimming.

2 There's a monster / a turtle in the sea.

3 Carrie Caretta can / can't move.

4 The animals want to help / watch Carrie.

4 Let's learn! Listen and say. •))

You must look left and right.

I must clean my teeth every day.
I mustn't make a mess in my room.
We must wash our hands before meals.
We mustn't eat lots of sweets.
You mustn't fight at school.
You mustn't play loud music.

5 Look and write must or mustn't.

1 You ___mustn't___ play football near the road.

2 Cars _____ stop at the traffic lights.

3 You _____ look left and right before you cross the road.

4 You _____ run across the road.

6 Sing along with the band! •))

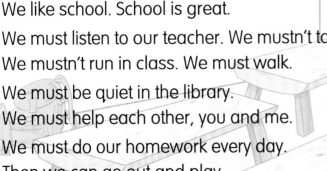

In our school there are rules.
They help us every day to work and to play.

School starts at eight. We mustn't be late.
We like school. School is great.

We must listen to our teacher. We mustn't talk.
We mustn't run in class. We must walk.

We must be quiet in the library.
We must help each other, you and me.

We must do our homework every day.
Then we can go out and play.

12b You're safe with us, Carrie.

1 Listen, point and say. 🔊

 fishermen

 ask

 safe

 kind

2 Listen and read. 🔊

1 Carrie is too far from the beach.

Look. There are some fishermen. They've got a boat. Let's ask them.

2 The fishermen want to help.

Can you help us, please?

Yes, we can help you.

3 Rob and Vicky dive into the sea.

Rob! Vicky! Be careful.

I'm tired.

Me too.

4 We've got her.

You're safe with us, Carrie.

Thank you. You're very kind.

3 Choose and write.

safe   boat   fishermen   ~~help~~

1 Everyone wants to ___help___ Carrie.
2 Tag sees some _____ .
3 They've got a _____ .
4 Carrie is _____ .

4 Let's learn! Listen and say. •))

> Look at us.
> We're friends.
> I like you.
> You like me.

> I like him.
> I like her.
> I like them.

5 Choose and write. Listen and check. •))

~~I / me~~   you   He / him   She / her   it   they / them

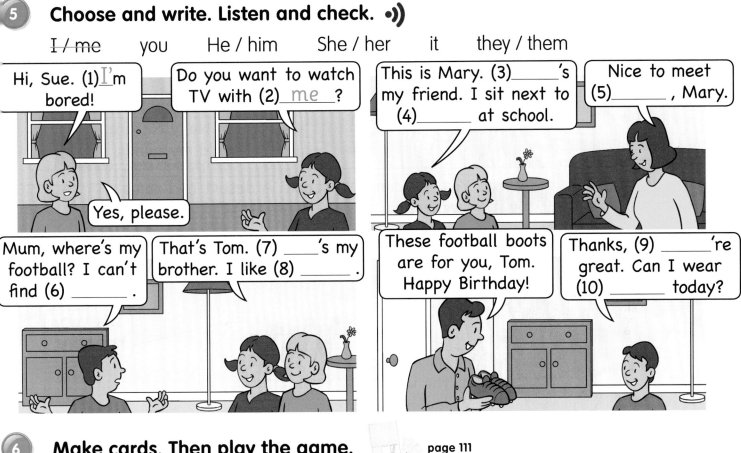

> Hi, Sue. (1) I'm bored!

> Do you want to watch TV with (2) me ?

> This is Mary. (3) _____'s my friend. I sit next to (4) _____ at school.

> Nice to meet (5) _____ , Mary.

> Yes, please.

> Mum, where's my football? I can't find (6) _____ .

> That's Tom. (7) _____'s my brother. I like (8) _____ .

> These football boots are for you, Tom. Happy Birthday!

> Thanks, (9) _____'re great. Can I wear (10) _____ today?

6 Make cards. Then play the game. page 111

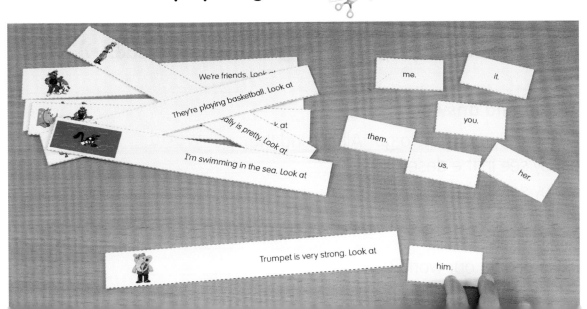

1 **Listen, point and say.** •))

2 **Listen and read.** •))

3 **Read again and answer.**

1 Where do the children want to go? All around the ___world___.
2 What do they see in the desert? _____
3 What do they see in the jungle? _____
4 Where is the snow? In the _____.
5 Where is the whale? In the _____.
6 Who must look after our world? _____

litter sky desert jungle ocean camel drop

4 **Choose and write.**

jungle   desert   ~~litter~~   hot   world   ocean

The children drop (1) _____litter_____ . Nelly Nature sees them. The children make a wish. They want to go all around the (2) _____ . They fly with Nelly. They see camels in the (3) _____ . It's (4) _____ there. They see parrots and monkeys in the rainy (5) _____ . They see mountains and snow. They see a big whale in the (6) _____ . It's amazing. They go home. They must look after their wonderful world.

5 **Listen again. Now you tell the story.** •))

How can we look after our world?

1 Listen, point and read. •))

a We live in one world, you and me, with mountains, deserts, forests, towns and seas. We must look after our wonderful world.

b We mustn't drop litter. We must put it in the bin. We can help to clean up our world. We can pick up litter in the park or on the beach.

1

c Water is very important. We mustn't waste water. We must save it. Turn off the water when you clean your teeth or wash the dishes. Have a shower, not a bath.

d We must be kind to animals. We must look after the fish and the birds, too. We can feed the birds with nuts and seeds in winter.

e We must think about other people. We must be quiet. We mustn't play loud music. We can use headphones to listen to music.

f We mustn't always go by car. We can sometimes walk or ride a bike to school. Or we can go by bus.

2 Listen and number. •))

3 **Read again and write** must **or** mustn't.

1 We ____mustn't____ drop litter.
2 We _____ save water.
3 We _____ always go by car.
4 We _____ be kind to animals.

5 We _____ play loud music.
6 We _____ look after our wonderful world.

4 **Do you look after our world? Tick or cross. Then ask and answer.**

	Me	My friend
Do you …		
1 put litter in the bin?		
2 walk or ride a bike to school?		
3 turn off the tap when you clean your teeth?		
4 use your headphones when you play music?		
5 look after your pet?		
6 feed the birds in the park?		

Key	4–6 ticks = Well done! You're helping to look after our world.
	2–3 ticks = Good. But you can do more.
	0–1 tick = Oh, dear! You aren't helping. You must help.

5 **Your project!** **Make a poster.**

OUR WONDERFUL WORLD

DO ✓ | DON'T ✗

Use your headphones

Put your litter in the bin

Don't play loud music

Don't waste water

Ride your bike to school

Don't drop litter

Review 6

1 **What can you see in the picture? Find and circle.**

(armbands)   sun cream   fishermen   bucket   spade
sandcastle   sun   video camera

2 **Listen and number.** •))

3 **Look at 2. Play the game.**

< Can I have an ice cream?   > You're number 1.

> Right.   My turn. I want to make a sandcastle. >

> You're 4.   Right. >

4 **Listen and chant.** •))

Hooray! It's a holiday today.
Let's play!

5   **Do the quiz.**

START

1. I want to _____.

2. _____ I _____ an ice cream, please?

3. You mustn't _____ litter.

4. Don't move. _____ there!

5. You _____ do your homework.

6. He's funny. Look at _____.

7. You _____ listen to your teacher.

8. She's swimming. Can you see _____?

9. Can you eat chocolates in bed? _____

10. We must put _____ in the bin.

11. You are kind. I like _____.

12. Can you ride your bike in the library? _____

13. I want to _____.

14. I want to make a _____.

15. You _____ talk in the library.

16. _____ I _____ a banana, please?

17. You _____ wear a hat on the beach.

18. You _____ play football in your bedroom.

19. They're in the boat. Can you see _____?

20. I'm the winner. Look at _____!

WELL DONE!

FINISH

105

Goodbye!

 Sing along with the band. •))

You can run in the park.
You can stay at home.
You can climb in the forests in the trees.
You can play on the beach.
You can laugh with your friends.
You can swim in the bright blue sea.

Summer holiday!
Summer holiday!
Goodbye, my friends, goodbye to you.
Summer holiday!
Summer holiday!
Goodbye from the animals in the zoo!

You can swim and dance.

You can skip and jump.

You can climb to the tops of the trees.

You can paint and draw.

You can read and dream.

You can dive in the bright blue sea.

Summer holiday!

Summer holiday!

Goodbye, my friends, goodbye to you.

Summer holiday!

Summer holiday!

Goodbye from the animals in the zoo!

The Yazoo

All:	Hello!
Sally:	Hello!
Child 1 (to Sally):	Hello! What's your name?
Sally:	My name is Sally.
Child 2:	Are you from England?
Sally:	Yes, I am.
All:	My name is … .
All:	We're from … .
All sing:	I'm from England. (Unit 1a)
Sally:	Here are my friends: Chatter, Trumpet, Tag, Karla and Patty.
Animals:	Hello! We're the animals in the zoo!
Child 3:	Do you like the zoo?
Chatter:	Yes, we do. Do you?
Children:	Yes, we do.
All sing:	Does Pandora like the zoo? (Unit 4a)
Trumpet:	I'm hungry.
Animals:	You're always hungry, Trumpet.
Children 4 & 5:	We're making a cake! You can help us!
All sing:	We're cooking in the kitchen. (Unit 5a)

Music Show

Child 6: I love cake! Delicious!

Child 7: Are there any sweets or chocolates?

Animals: Let's look in the kitchen.

All sing: There are some apples in the bowl. (Unit 8a)

Tag (to children): Were you at school yesterday?

Children: Yes, we were.

Child 8: I talked to all my friends.

Child 9: I played basketball. It was fun.

All sing: Yesterday I walked to school. (Unit 10a)

Tag: Can we go out and play now, Sally?

Sally: You must do your homework first.

Children: We do our homework every day. Then we can play.

All sing: In our school there are rules. (Unit 12a)

Karla: Now it's summer and we don't go to school in summer.

All: Hurray!

Karla: What do we do in summer?

All: We go on holiday.

All sing: You can run in the park. (Goodbye!)

International Friendship Day

1 **Listen, point and say.** •))

 friend   laugh   share   kind

2 **Listen, read and match.** •))

1 I'm helping my friend. We're making a poster.

2 We're laughing together. We're having a party.

3 We're sharing. We're eating pizza.

4 We're playing volleyball together. We're having fun.

HAPPY FRIENDSHIP DAY

1

3 **Listen and sing.** •))

Friends, friends,
it's Friendship Day!
Let's laugh and play together.
Friends, friends,
it's Friendship Day.
Let's love and help each other.

You're my friend.
You make me smile.
You help me every day.
You're kind.
You share your toys with me.
We smile and laugh and play.

4 **Make a Friendship Day poster.**

Carnival

1 Listen, point and say. •))

mask

streamers

costume

throw

dance

2 Listen, read and match. •))

1 This is me. I'm going to a carnival with my sisters. I'm wearing a clown costume and a big hat. It's red, yellow and blue. My little sister is wearing a clown costume, too.

2 Look at these people. They're at the Notting Hill Carnival. They're dancing to the music. They're wearing beautiful costumes.

3 We're at a party. We're laughing and having fun. There are lots of balloons and streamers.

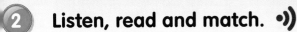

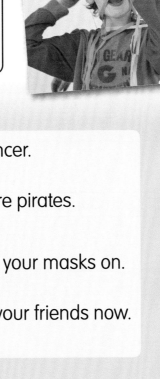

3 Listen and sing. •))

I'm a cowboy, you're a dancer.
Happy Carnival to you!
We are clowns and they are pirates.
Happy Carnival to you!

Throw your streamers, put your masks on.
Happy Carnival to you!
Dance and laugh with all your friends now.
Happy Carnival to you!

4 Make a carnival mask.

Festivals in Britain

1 Listen, point and say the months. •))

2 Listen, read and point. •))

January	February	March	April
New Year's Day	Pancake Day	Mother's Day	Easter
May	**June**	**July**	**August**
May Day	Father's Day	School holidays	Notting Hill Carnival
September	**October**	**November**	**December**
Harvest Festival	Hallowe'en	Bonfire night	Christmas

3 Look at 2. Ask and answer.

When is New Year's Day?   It's in January.

4 Answer for you.

1 When is your birthday?

2 What's your favourite month? Why?

5 Make your own calendar.

112